The Hollow Crown

An entertainment by and about the Kings and Queens of England

Music, Poetry, Speeches, Letters and other Writings from the Chronicles, from Plays, and in the Monarch's own words - also Music concerning them and by them

Devised by
JOHN BARTON

Samuel French — London
New York - Toronto - Hollywood

ISBN 0 573 01183 4

Please see page viii for further copyright information

THE HOLLOW CROWN

First presented by the Royal Shakespeare Theatre at the Aldwych Theatre, London, on 19th March 1961 with:

MAX ADRIAN
JOHN BARTON
RICHARD JOHNSON
DOROTHY TUTIN
RICHARD GOLDING (Bass)
KEVIN MILLER (Tenor)
ERIC SHILLING (Baritone)
JAMES WALKER (Harpsichord and piano)

The following members of the Royal Shakespeare Company have also taken part in subsequent performances of *The Hollow Crown*:

PEGGY ASHCROFT
TONY CHURCH
DEREK GODFREY
MARIUS GORING
PAUL HARDWICK
GERALDINE McEWAN
ANTHONY NICHOLL
VANESSA REDGRAVE
OLIVE SWIFT

THE READERS

The various items are shared between four readers, one woman and three men. A suggested allocation of the men's passages is made below, but they may, of course, be re-allocated to suit the capacity of individual readers, provided that no reader reads two adjacent items. The voices and personalities of the readers should be as contrasted as possible, e.g.

READER A (who begins and ends each part) should if possible be older than the other two men and covers the most comic and sophisticated items.

READER B (the woman) should have a wide vocal range and be able to represent characters as widely differentiated as a girl of fifteen and an old lady of seventy.

READER C should have a warm and deepish voice and covers the more bluff and extroverted passages.

READER D covers the more detached, ironic and intellectual passages.

THE MUSIC

Four musicians are used: a BASS, a BARITONE, a TENOR, and an ACCOMPANIST who can play both the harpsichord and the piano.

The Music is available on hire from Sammuel French Ltd.

ARRANGEMENT OF THE STAGE

The four READERS' chairs should be set about two feet apart from one another. It is desirable that they should each have arms to them, especially numbers 2 and 3, in order to facilitate reading. Their style should be as indeterminate in period as possible.

A small table, about a foot high, should be placed in front of the READERS' chairs, close enough to be easily within reach, but allowing enough space for the READERS to move behind it. On it should be pre-set a water carafe, four glasses, and a quill pen. For Part II the quill should be pre-set on the downstage corner of the piano.

The three SINGERS' chairs should be of the same design as the READERS' chairs. It is desirable that the chair seats and the tops of the two stools should be covered with the same material, preferably scarlet in colour.

The lectern should be fairly light, so that it can be moved about easily, and not too high, so that the READERS can easily be seen when standing behind it. The various positions in which it is used are marked on the plan on page vii, e.g.—(i)—.

A plain carpet of some light colour should be used to cover the main acting area, i.e. it should be set slightly off-centre towards prompt.

STAGING

Unless otherwise indicated by the stage directions, an individual item should be read seated. Main moves are set out in the stage-directions, but READERS may find it helpful to make a few subsidiary moves during items which are performed standing.

The READERS should know their parts well enough to be able to look up from their scripts even if they have not learnt individual passages. It is important, however, that certain items should be learnt by heart as they cannot easily be put over or brought alive if they are merely read. These are marked below with an asterisk—*. The READERS should still hold their books for the learnt items, so that the convention of a dramatic reading is maintained throughout.

The ensemble songs should be sung in front of the piano with the SINGERS forming a diagonal line rather than facing straight out to the audience (see Stage Plan). In the ensembles the TENOR should be nearest the harpsichord, the BARITONE in the middle, and the BASS farthest onstage.

LIGHTING

Until the last three items of the programme, there need be no lighting changes. A strong general lighting should be used, with a focus on the READERS' chairs and in front of the piano. The MUSICIANS' should be underlit.

Cue 1 (after the BALLAD BY PRINCE ALBERT) is to take down the light on the READERS' chairs and strengthen it in the area behind the harpsichord so as to concentrate the light on READER B while she reads the passage from QUEEN VICTORIA'S JOURNAL (10 seconds cross-fade).

Cue 2 (after the BEETHOVEN VARIATIONS) is to take down the light in the area of the piano and harpsichord and over the whole stage area, leaving a localised focus on chairs 2, 3 and 4 for the passage from THE MORTE D'ARTHUR (15 seconds cross-fade).

Cue 3 (ten seconds) is to take out all light except downstage centre, so that READER A is spot-lit as he speaks the final paragraph in the performance.

Cue 4 is for a three-second fade to black-out at the end of the MORTE D'ARTHUR passage.

Cue 5 is to restore the full-stage lighting for the company to take their curtain calls.

PROGRAMME COPY

The programme copy should follow the lay-out shown on pages ix to xii. Sufficient light should be left on in the auditorium to enable the audience to identify individual items in their programmes.

COSTUME

The men wear dinner jackets. The woman should wear a long evening dress, preferably black, with a coloured stole which can be draped in different ways according to the part she is playing.

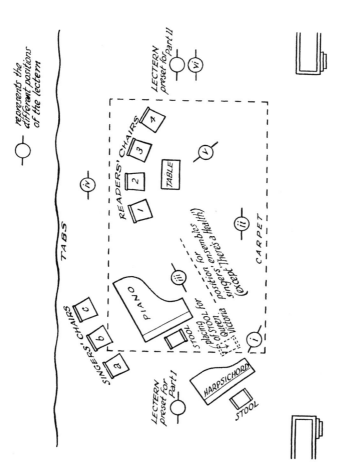

TABS

represents the different positions of the lectern

SINGERS' CHAIRS

a   b   c

LECTERN preset for Part I

HARPSICHORD

STOOL

PIANO

STOOL

placing of STOOL for queen Victoria

position for ensembles (except 'There's a Health' singers)

READERS' CHAIRS

1   2   3   4

TABLE

CARPET

LECTERN preset for Part II

vii

ix

THE MONARCHS SPEAK FOR THEMSELVES
HENRY V—Agincourt Song

Drama
EDWARD III writes a love-letter to the Countess of Sallisbury. *William Shakespeare*

The Queene's Command—Orlando Gibbons

Diplomacy
HENRY VII sends a secret memorandum to his Ambassadors concerning a proposed marriage between himself and the Queen of Naples, and they reply to it.

A Speech
MARY denounces the rebellion of Sir Thomas Wyatt, raised in protest against her proposed marriage to Philip of Spain.

HENRY VIII—The King's Hunt

Letters
HENRY VIII proposes to Anne Boleyn, a lady in waiting at his court.
ANNE BOLEYN writes to Henry from the Tower before her execution.

Song by ANNE BOLEYN's brother
"Oh, Death, rock her asleep"

Poems
HENRY VI   "Kingdoms are but cares"
HENRY VIII   "As the Holly groweth green"
ELIZABETH complains of being importuned with love
CHARLES II "I pass all my hours in a shady old grove"

CHARLES II—"Here's a Health unto his Majesty"

PART TWO

The Stuarts

JAMES I blows a Counterblast to Tobacco

CHARLES I confronts JOHN BRADSHAW, President
of the Court, at his trial for high treason and is
condemned to death.

Ayre by CHARLES I

CHARLES II (1) marries Catharine of Braganza (from
a speech to Parliament and two letters to the Lord
Chancellor)
(2) is anatomised by the Marquis of Halifax, one of
his ministers.

The Vicar of Bray upholds the Protestant Succession

CHARLES II	WILLIAM AND MARY
JAMES II	ANNE
GEORGE I	

The Illustrious House of Hanover

QUEEN CAROLINE	The death of George II's Wife	*Lord Hervey*
GEORGE II	is buried in Westminster Abbey	*Horace Walpole*
GEORGE III	discusses the Arts with the novelist and diarist	*Fanny Burney*
GEORGE IV	is unswathed and interpreted	*William Thackeray*
THE REGENCY	The madness of GEORGE III	*Marianne Thornton to E. M. Forster*
WILLIAM IV	makes a good start	*The Greville Memoirs*

The Victorian Age

A Ballad to an Absent Friend
by ALBERT, Prince Consort
(with words by his brother, ERNEST)

VICTORIA   describes her Coronation at the
age of nineteen
(from her Private Journal)
Variations on God Save the King—Beethoven

EPILOGUE
From the MORTE D'ARTHUR *by Sir Thomas
Malory*

PART ONE

The READERS *enter down left; the* MUSICIANS *down right. After bowing together in the centre of the stage, all except* READER A *take their seats in the following order:* ACCOMPANIST *on stool at harpsichord,* TENOR *in chair* (*a*), BARITONE *in chair* (*b*), BASS *in chair* (*c*), READER B *in chair* 2, READER C *in chair* 3, READER D *in chair* 4.

PROLOGUE*

READER A

For God's sake let us sit upon the ground,
And tell sad stories of the death of kings—
How some have been deposed, some slain in war,
Some haunted by the ghosts they have deposed,
Some poisoned by their wives, some sleeping killed;
All murdered—for within the Hollow Crown
That rounds the mortal temples of a king,
Keeps Death his court; and there the antic sits,
Scoffing his state and grinning at his pomp,
Allowing him a breath, a little scene,
To monarchize, be feared, and kill with looks,
Infusing him with self and vain conceit,
As if this flesh which walls about our life,
Were brass impregnable: and humoured thus,
Comes at last, and with a little pin
Bores through his castle wall, and farewell king!

(READER A *sits in chair* 1)

3

THE DEATH OF KINGS

READER D

After the birth-tide of our Lord Jesus Christ one thousand seven and eighty winters, in the one and twentieth year of his governance in England, the King fell sick of the evil and died. This WILLIAM was for certain a wise and a mighty prince. We may not well forget the good peace he made in this land; for a man might fare throughout the realm without let or hindrance in his time, and with his bosom full of gold. But, alas, how false and fleeting is the wealth of this world. He who was sometime a most high King and lord of lands had now from all his lands no greater measure than some seven foot, and no richer mantle than a little mould.

(READER D *moves towards centre*)

KING WILLIAM, THE SECOND of that name, was of person a square man, red-coloured, his forehead foursquare like a window. He was changeable, inconstant, covetous and cruel, ever tormenting his people with taxes and with armies. Wherefore he was hateful to his people and loathed of God; to which his end bore witness, for it was an unhallowed end and sudden. For on the morning after Lammas day, hunting in the New Forest in Hampshire, he was struck by an arrow all unawares and fell down stark dead, and never spake word. Wherefore they laid his body upon a collier's cart, which one silly lean beast bore surly into the City of Winchester.

(READER D *moves left*)

So after he was buried, his Council chose his brother HENRY for to be King, who straight vowed to abate each several ill that his brother had ill done before him. This Henry was a noble prince, strong and mighty of body, well in flesh, and a merry. No man dared wrong another in his time, and whosoever would carry his load of gold and silver about the land, no man dared venture anything but good to him.

Yet howsoever the King himself had gathered gold and silver, no good did men do for his soul therewith: for KING STEPHEN, that came after, lightly laid hands on his treasure and as lightly consumed it.

In this King's time there was nothing but strife and evil in the land. For when they perceived that he was a mild and soft and good man and did no justice, the lords all wondered at it. And though they had done him homage and sworn oaths, they kept no troth, but were all forsworn and their troth all broken. For each lord built a castle for himself, and held his castle boldly against the King, so that the land was full of castles.

Then seized they many a person, both men and women, and put them in their castles, and tortured them for gold and silver. And never were martyrs tortured so as they were. For they were hung by the feet and smoked with foul smoke, and hung by the thumbs or head with coats of mail hanging heavy upon their feet. Knotted cords were put about their heads and twisted till it went to the brain. And there was never seen such hanging.

And so it lasted for nineteen years while Stephen was King, till the land was all undone and darkened with such deeds, and men said openly that Christ and his angels slept.

(READER D *returns to chair* 4)

5

(The BASS *stands by the upstage centre end of the piano, facing down left)*

WORLDES BLISS

BASS

Worldes bliss lasteth no throw,
It wilts and wends away anon.
The longer that I it know,
The less I find price therein.
For all it is mingled with care,
With sorrow and with evil fare,
And at the last poor and bare.
It let man ween it gaineth agony.
All the bliss thus here and there,
Belongeth at the end weeping and moaning.

(The BASS *returns to chair centre)*

6

QUEEN ELEANOR'S CONFESSION

READER A

Queen Eleanor was a sick woman,
  And afraid that she should die;
Then she sent for two friars of France,
  For to speak with them speedily.

The King called down his nobles all,
  By one, by two, and by three;
"Earl Martial, I'll go shrive the Queen,
  And thou shalt wend with me!"

"A boon, a boon!" quoth Earl Martial,
  And fell on his bended knee,
"That whatsoe'er the Queen may say,
  No harm thereof may be."

"I'll pawn my living and my lands,
  My sceptre and my crown,
That whate'er Queen Eleanor says,
  I will not write it down.

Do you put on one friar's coat,
  And I'll put on another,
And we'll to Queen Eleanor go,
  One friar like another."

Thus both attiréd then they go;
  When they came to Whitehall,
The bells they did ring, and the quiristers sing,
  And the torches did light them all.

When that they came before the Queen,
    They fell on their bended knee:
"Are you two friars of France?" she said,
    "Which I suppose you be."

"We are two friars of France," they said,
    "As you suppose we be;
We have not been at any mass
    Since we came from the sea."

"The first vile thing that ere I did
    To you I'll not deny;
I made a box of poison strong,
    To poison King Henry."

"That is a vile sin," then said the King,
    "God may forgive it thee!"
"Amen! Amen!" quoth Earl Martial,
    "And I wish it so may be."

"The next vile thing that ere I did
    To you I will discover;
I poisonéd Fair Rosamund,
    All in fair Woodstock bower."

"That is a vile sin," then said the King,
    "God may forgive it thee!"
"Amen! Amen!" quoth Earl Martial,
    "And I wish it so may be."

"The next vile thing that ere I did
    I will to you unfold;
Earl Martial had my maidenhead,
    Underneath this cloth of gold."

"That is a vile sin," then said the king,
    "God may forgive it thee!"
"Amen! Amen!" quoth Earl Martial,—
    With a heavy heart then spoke *he*.

8

"Do you see yonders little boy,
    A tossing of that ball?
That is Earl Martial's eldest son,
    And I love him the best of all.

Do you see yonders little boy,
    A catching of the ball?
That is King Henry's son," she said,
    "And I love him the worst of all.

His head is like unto a bull,
    His nose is like a boar."
"No matter for that," King Henry said,
    "I love him the better therefore."

The King pull'd off his friar's coat,
    And appearéd all in red;
She shrieked and she cried, she wrung her hands,
    And said she was betrayed.

The King looked o'er his left shoulder,
    And a grim look lookéd he,
And said, "Earl Martial, but for my oath,
    Then hangéd shouldst thou be."

(READER A *returns to chair* 1)

9

FROM 16TH AND 17TH CENTURY CHRONICLERS

READER C

THE SECOND HENRY was somewhat red of face, and broad breasted, short of body, and therewithal fat, which made him use much exercise. He was out of measure given to fleshly lust; for not contented with the use of his wife, he kept many concubines. But namely he delighted most in the company of a pleasant damsel, whom he called the rose of the world (the common people named her Rosamund) for her passing beauty, being verily a rare and peerless piece in those days. He made her an house at Woodstock in Oxfordshire, like a labyrinth, that no creature might find her or come to her except he were instructed by the King. But the common report of the people is that the queen in the end found her out by a silken thread, which the King had drawn after him out of her chamber with his foot, and dealt with her in such sharp and cruel wise, that she lived not long thereafter.

She was buried at Godstow, in an house of Nuns, with these verses upon her tomb:

The rose of the world, but not the clean flower,
Is now here graven, to whom beauty was lent.
In this grave, full dark, is now her bower,
That by her life was sweet and redolent.
But now that she is from this life blent,
Though she were sweet, now foully doth she stink,
A mirror, good, for all men that on her think.

(READER C *rises and moves down centre*)

RICHARD I was big of stature, with a merry countenance, fair and comely; of hair bright auburn, of long arms, and nimble in his joints; to his soldiers favourable, bountiful to his friends, to strangers a grievous enemy; so that not without cause he obtained the surname of *Coeur de Lion*; was, liberal, merciful, just, and, which is most of all, religious. A prince born for the good of Christendom.

(READER C *moves right*)

This Richard being dead, Prince JOHN became his successor. He was something fat, of a sour and angry countenance. Naturally he loved his ease, yet his fortune was to be ever in action. He was all by fits, intemperate in his best temper, but when distempered with sickness most intemperate of all—as appeared at his last, when, being sick of a fever, he would needs be eating raw peaches and drinking sweet ale. He most miserably departed this life, deprived of all his treasures, and not retaining the smallest portion of his land in peace, so that he was truly called *Lackland*. He was wrapped in a monk's cowl and so laid in his grave.

(READER C *moves centre*)

But to let pass this cold discourse of a coffin of bones covered with clods of clay, you shall understand that he did yet morally survive in his son HENRY III, the father of as valiant Kings as any we had. He was of stature but mean, yet well-compacted; of stomach rather noble than stout. His most eminent virtue, and that which made him the more eminent, as being rare among princes, was his continency.

But now to conclude with the noble prince KING EDWARD THE FIRST. He was tall of stature, higher than an ordinary person by head and shoulders, and therefore called *Longshank*; swarthy, strong of body, but lean; his eyes in his anger sparkling like fire. Concerning his conditions, as he was in war peaceful, so in peace he was warlike. In continency of life he was equal to his father, in acts of valour far beyond him. Yet he was not only valiant, but politic, labouring to bring this divided isle into one entire monarchy, which he was very near to have achieved.

(Reader C moves down stage a little)

*But, alas, of four sons which he had, three of them died in his own life-time, who were worthy to have outlived him, and the fourth, Edward, the Second of that name, outlived him, who was worthy never to have been born. For this prince lived not only to be overthrown by his indignant peers, but was eventually slain by one of them, and that in most cruel wise.

(Reader D rises and sits in chair 3)

(Reader C sits in chair 4)

(The BARITONE *rises and moves in the bay of the piano facing down right)*

BALLADE BY RICHARD I

BARITONE

No one will tell me the cause of my sorrow,
Why they have made me a prisoner here
Wherefore with dolour I now make my moan;
Friends had I many but help have I none
Shameful it is that they leave me to ransom,
To languish here two winters long.

(The BARITONE *moves downstage round the piano and returns to chair (b))*

13

THE DEPOSITION OF RICHARD II BY HENRY BOLINBROKE

READER D

In the mean season, while the king sat at dinner, who did eat but little (his heart was so full that he had no lust to eat), all the country about his castle was full of men of war. Then he demanded of his cousin, Henry Bolinbroke, what men they were that appeared so many in the fields.

"What would they have?" quoth the king. "They will have you," quoth the earl, "and bring you to London and put you in the Tower; there is none other remedy, ye can scape none otherwise." "No?" quoth the king, and he was sore afraid of those words, and said, "Cousin, can you not provide for my surety? I will not gladly put me into their hands." Then the earl said, "Sir, I see none other remedy, but to yield yourself as my prisoner; and when they know that ye be my prisoner, they will do you no hurt."

Then the king, who saw himself in a hard case, yielded himself prisoner to the earl of Derby, and bound himself and promised to do all that he would have him to do. Then many men of arms and archers entered the castle. Then the earl of Derby caused a cry to be made, on pain of death no man to be so hardy to take away anything within the castle, nor to lay hands upon any person, for all were under the earl's safe-guard and protection: which cry was kept, no man durst break it.

And as it was informed me, King Richard had a greyhound called Math, who always waited upon the king and would know no man else; for whensoever the king did ride, he that kept the greyhound did let him loose and he would straight run to the king and fawn upon him and leap with his fore feet upon the king's shoulders.

(READER D *rises and moves down centre*)

And as the king and the earl of Derby talked together in the court, the greyhound, who was wont to leap upon the king, left the king and came to the earl of Derby, Duke of Lancaster, and made to him the same friendly countenance and cheer as he was wont to do to the king. The duke, who knew not the greyhound, demanded of the king what the greyhound would do.

"Cousin," quoth the king, "It is a great good token to you and an evil sign to me." "Sir, how know you that?" quoth the duke. "I know it well;" quoth the king, "The greyhound maketh you cheer this day as king of England, as ye shall be, and I shall be deposed. The greyhound hath this knowledge naturally: therefore take him to you; he will follow you and forsake me."

The duke understood well those words and cherished the greyhound, who would never after follow King Richard, but followed the Duke of Lancaster.

(READER D *returns to chair* 3)

FROM JANE AUSTEN'S HISTORY OF ENGLAND

READER B

THE HISTORY OF ENGLAND, by a Partial, Prejudiced and Ignorant Historian.

HENRY THE FOURTH ascended the throne of England much to his own satisfaction in the year 1399, having prevailed on his cousin and predecessor RICHARD THE SECOND to resign it to him, and to retire for the rest of his life to Pomfret Castle, where he happened to be murdered. Be this as it may, King HENRY did not live for ever either; but falling ill, his son the Prince of Wales came and took away the crown; whereupon the King made a long speech, for which I must refer the Reader to Shakespeare's Play.

Things being thus settled between them the King died, and was succeeded by his son HENRY, who grew quite *reformed* and *amiable*, forsaking all his dissipated companions. His Majesty then turned his thoughts to France, where he went and fought the famous Battle of Agincourt. He afterwards married the King's daughter Catherine, a very *agreeable* woman by Shakespeare's account. In spite of all this however, he died, and was succeeded by his son, HENRY VI.

I cannot say much for this Monarch's *sense*. Nor would I if I could, for he was a Lancastrian. It was in this reign that Joan of Arc lived and made such a *row* among the English. They should not have *burnt* her—but they did.

EDWARD THE FOURTH. This Monarch was famous only for his Beauty and his Courage, and he showed his undaunted behaviour in marrying one woman while he was engaged to another. One of his mistresses was Jane Shore, who has had a play written about her, but it is a tragedy and therefore not worth reading.

His Majesty was succeeded by his son, EDWARD V. This unfortunate Prince lived so little a while that nobody had time even to draw his picture. He was murdered by his Uncle's Contrivance, whose name was RICHARD THE THIRD.

The character of this Prince has in general been very *severely* handled by *Historians*. But as he was a *York*, *I* am rather inclined to suppose him a very *respectable* Man. It has been confidently asserted that he killed his two nephews, but it has also been asserted that he did *not* kill his two nephews, which I am inclined to believe true. Whether innocent or guilty, he did not reign long in peace, for HENRY TUDOR, Earl of Richmond, as great a villain as ever lived, made a great fuss about getting the Crown, and having killed the King at the battle of Bosworth, he succeeded to it.

His eldest daughter, however, was married to the King of Scotland and had the happiness of being the grandmother to one of the first Characters in the World. But of *her*, I shall have occasion to speak more at large in future. His Majesty was succeeded by his son Henry whose only merit was his not being *quite* so bad as his daughter Elizabeth.

The Crimes and Cruelties of HENRY VIII are too numerous to be mentioned, and nothing can be said in his vindication, but that his abolishing Religious Houses and leaving them to the ruinous depredations of time has been of infinite use to the landscape of England in general, which was probably a principal motive for his doing it, since otherwise why should a Man who was of no Religion himself be at so much trouble to abolish one which had for ages been established in the Kingdom?

EDWARD VI. As this prince was only nine years old at the time of his Father's death, the Duke of

Somerset was chosen Protector of the Realm during his minority. The Duke was on the whole a very amiable Character, and is somewhat of a favourite with me. He was beheaded; of which he might with reason have been proud, had he known that such was the death of Mary Queen of Scotland.

MARY TUDOR. I cannot pity the Kingdom for the misfortunes they experienced during her Reign, since they fully deserved them, for having allowed her to succeed her Brother—which was a double piece of folly, since they might have foreseen that as she died without children, she would be succeeded by that pest to society, that disgrace to humanity, ELIZABETH.

It was the peculiar misfortune of this Woman to have had Ministers. I know that it has been asserted and believed that Lord Burleigh, Sir Francis Walsingham and the rest were deserving, experienced, and able Ministers. But oh! how blinded such writers and such Readers must be to true merit, to merit despised, neglected, and defamed, if they can persist in such opinions when they reflect that these men, these boasted men, were such scandals to their country and to their sex as to allow and assist their Queen in confining for the space of nineteen years, a Woman who had every reason to expect assistance and protection; and at length allowed Elizabeth to bring this *amiable* Woman to an untimely, unmerited, and scandalous Death. She was executed in the Great Hall at Fotheringay Castle (sacred Place!) on Wednesday, the 8th of February, 1587—to the everlasting Reproach of Elizabeth, her Ministers, and of England in general.

JAMES THE FIRST. Though this King had some faults, on the whole I cannot help *liking* him. He was a Roman Catholic, and as I am myself partial to the Roman Catholic religion, it is with infinite regret that I am obliged to blame the Behaviour of any Member of it: yet Truth, being I think very *excusable* in a *Historian*, I am necessitated to say that in this reign, the

Roman Catholics of England did not behave like *Gentlemen* to the Protestants.

CHARLES I. The events of this Monarch's reign are too numerous for my pen, and indeed the recital of any events is uninteresting to me; my principle reasons for undertaking the History of England were to abuse Elizabeth (though I am rather fearful of having fallen off in that part of my scheme), and to prove the innocence of the Queen of Scotland, which I flatter myself with having effectually done.

(READER B *returns to chair* 2)

19

(The three SINGERS *move via the on-stage side of the piano and line up in front of it; the* TENOR *right, the* BARITONE *in the middle and the* BASS *left.)*

AGINCOURT SONG

TENOR, BARITONE AND BASS

Our King went forth to Normandy
With grace and might and chivalry;
The God for him wrought marvellously.
Whereof England may call and cry:
    Deo gracias.
    Deo gracias Anglia,
    Redde pro victoria.

The gracious God now save our King,
His people and all his well-willing,
Give him good life and good ending
That we with mirth may safely sing:
    Deo gracias.
    Deo gracias Anglia,
    Redde pro victoria.

(The SINGERS *return to their chairs via the off-stage side of the piano and sit,* BASS *in chair (a),* BARITONE *in chair (b),* TENOR *in chair (c))*

EDWARD III WRITES A LOVE LETTER TO THE COUNTESS OF SALISBURY*

READER C AS THE KING

READER A AS LODOWICK

KING Now: hast thou pen and paper ready, Lodowick?

LODOWICK Ready, my liege.

KING Then in this summer arbour sit by me;
Since green our thoughts, green be the conventicle.

(READER C *leans against the piano*)

Now Lodowick, invocate some golden Muse
To bring thee hither some enchanted pen,
And when thou writ'st my tears, encouch the word
Before and after with such sweet laments,
That it may raise drops in a Tartar's eye,
And make a flintheart Scythian pitiful;
For so much moving hath a poet's pen.

LODOWICK To whom, my lord, shall I direct my style?

KING To one that shames the fair and sots the wise.
Better than beautiful thou must begin;
Devise for fair a fairer word than fair,
And every ornament that thou wouldst praise,
Fly it a pitch above the soar of praise,
Begin; I will to contemplate the while.

LODOWICK Write I to a woman?

KING What, thinkst thou I did bid thee praise a horse?

LODOWICK Of what condition or estate she is,
'Twere requisite that I should know, my lord.

KING Of such estate, that hers is as a throne,
And my estate the foot-stool where she treads.

(READER C *moves to the on-stage corner of the harpsichord*)

Write on, while I peruse her in my thoughts.
Her voice to music or the nightingale—
But why should I speak of the nightingale?
The nightingale singeth of adulterate wrong,
And that, compared, is too satirical.
Her hair, far softer than the silk-worm's twist,
Like to a flattering glass, doth make more fair
The yellow Amber. "Like a flattering glass"
Comes in too soon; for, writing of her eyes,
I'll say that like a glass they catch the sun,
And thence the hot reflection doth rebound
Against my breast, and burns my heart within.
Come, Lodowick, hast thou turned thy ink to gold?
Read, lord, read.

(READER C *moves upstage towards the piano*)

LODOWICK "More fair and chaste than is the Queen
of shades . . ."

KING That line hath two faults, gross and palpable:
Compar'st thou her to the pale queen of night,
Who, being set in dark, seems therefore light?
What is she, when the sun lifts up his head,
But like a fading taper, dim and dead?

LODOWICK What is the other fault, my Sovereign?

KING Read o'er the line again.

LODOWICK "More fair and chaste" . . .

KING I did not bid thee talk of chastity!
Out with the moon line, I will none of it.
And let me have her likened to the sun,
Who smiles upon the basest weed that grows
As lovingly as on the fragrant rose.
Let's see what follows that same moonlight line.

LODOWICK "More fair and chaste than is the queen
of shades,
More bold in constancy . . ."

22

KING In constancy! Than who?

LODOWICK ". . . than Judith was."

KING Blot, blot, good Lodowick. Let us hear the rest.

(READER A *rises*)

LODOWICK There's all that yet is done.

KING I thank thee, thou has done little ill.
No, love can sound but well in lovers' tongues;
Give me the pen and paper: *I* will write.

(READER C *crosses to* READER A
and takes the quill from him.
READER A *crosses and sits in chair*
4. READER C *sits in chair* 1)

THE QUEENE'S COMMAND

Played on the Harpsichord by the
ACCOMPANIST

HENRY VII
INVESTIGATES A POSSIBLE
MARRIAGE

READER D AS THE KING

READER A AS HIS AMBASSADORS

KING Instructions given by the King's Highness to his trusty and well beloved servants, showing how they shall order themselves when they shall come to the presence of the old Queen of Naples and the young Queen, her daughter.

First, they shall note and mark the young Queen's *discretion, wisdom,* and *gravity* in her communication and answer in every behalf.

AMBASSADORS At our coming to the said Queens we kneeled down before them and kissed their hands, and delivered my Lady Princess's letters unto them. First, the old Queen answered for herself as a noble, wise woman; and after the young Queen with a *sad* and a *noble* countenance, and with great *discretion,* uttered and spake such words as pleased her, not having *many words* but full steadfast, and with no high speech. The old Queen had the like words, and many more.

KING Item, specially to note the stature of the said young Queen, and the features of her body.

AMBASSADORS As to this article, the *stature* of the said young Queen we cannot perfectly understand nor know, for commonly when that we came unto her presence her grace was sitting on a pillow. And as to the *features* of her body, forasmuch as that at all times that we have seen her grace ever, she had a great *mantle of cloth* on her, in such wise after the manner of that country that a man shall not lightly perceive anything except only the visage, wherefore we could not be in certain of any features of her body.

KING Item, specially to mark the favour of the young Queen's visage, whether she be painted or not, and whether it be fat or lean, sharp or round, and whether her countenance be cheerful and amiable, frowning or melancholy, steadfast or light, or blushing in communication.

AMBASSADORS As to this article, as far as that we can perceive or know, the said Queen is *not* painted, and the favour of her visage is *amiable*, and somewhat round and fat, not frowning, but steadfast, and with a demure womanly shamefaced countenance, and of few words. And we think that she uttered the fewer words by cause the Queen her mother was present, which had all the sayings.

KING Item, to mark well the fashion of her nose.

AMBASSADORS As to this article, the fashion of her nose is a little rising in the midward and a little coming or bowing towards the end. And she is much like nosed unto her mother.

KING Item, to mark whether there appear any hair about her lips or not.

AMBASSADORS As to this article, as far as we can perceive and see, the said Queen hath no hair appearing about her lips or mouth.

KING Item, to mark her breasts and paps, whether they be big or small.

AMBASSADORS As to this article, the said Queen's breasts be somewhat great and fully, and inasmuch as that they were trussed somewhat high, after the manner of the country, the which causeth her grace for to seem much the fullyer, and her neck to be the shorter.

KING Item, that they endeavour them to speak with the said young Queen fasting, and to approach as

25

near to her mouth as they honestly may, to the intent that they may feel the condition of her breath, whether it be sweet or not, and to mark every time when they speak with her if they feel any savour of spices, rosewater, or musk by the breath of her mouth.

AMBASSADORS To this article: we could never come unto the speech of the said Queen fasting, wherefore we could nor might not attain to knowledge of that part of this article, notwithstanding at such other times as we have spoken with the said Queen, we have approached as nigh unto her visage as that conveniently we might do, and we could feel no savour of any spices or waters, and we think verily by the cleanness of her complexion and of her mouth that the said Queen is like for to be of a *sweet savour*, and well aired.

KING Item, the King's said servants shall also diligently inquire for some cunning painter to the intent that the said painter may draw a picture of the said young Queen. And in case they may perceive that the painter hath not made a perfect similitude and likeness, or that he hath omitted any feature or circumstance, then they shall cause the same painter so often times to renew and reform the same picture till it be made perfect.

(READER C *rises*)

READER C There is no answer made to this article.

(READERS A *and* C *return to chairs* 4 *and* 1)

26

(The BASS *rises and sets the lectern in position (i)
beside the harpsichord)*

*(*READER B *rises, crosses to the lectern and places her
script upon it. The* BASS *bows to her and returns to his
chair)*

FROM A SPEECH MADE IN THE GUILDHALL BY MARY TUDOR

READER B

I am come unto you in mine own person to tell you
that which already you see and know; that is, how
traitorously and rebelliously a number of Kentishmen
have assembled themselves against us and you. Their
pretence was for a *Marriage* determined for us, to the
which, and to all the articles thereof, ye have been made
privy. But they have arrogantly and traitorously demanded to have the governance of our person, the
keeping of the Tower, and the placing of our council-
lors.

Now, loving subjects, what I am ye right well know.
I am your Queen, to whom at my coronation, you
promised your allegiance and obedience, and therefore
I doubt not that ye will not suffer a vile traitor to have
the order and governance of our person, and to occupy
our estate, especially being so vile a traitor as Wyatt is.

And I say to you on the word of a prince, I cannot tell
how naturally the mother loveth the child, for I was
never the mother of any. But certainly, if a prince and
governor may as naturally and earnestly love her subjects as the mother doth love the child, then assure
yourselves that I, being your lady and mistress, do as
earnestly and tenderly love and favour you. And I, thus
loving you, cannot but think that ye as heartily and
faithfully love me: and then I doubt not but that we
shall give these rebels a short and speedy overthrow.

As concerning the marriage, ye shall understand that
I enterprised not the doing thereof without advice, and

27

that by the advice of all our Privy Council. And as touching myself, I assure you, I am not so bent to my will, neither so precise nor affectionate, that for mine own pleasure I would choose where I lust. For God, I thank him, to whom be the praise therefore, I have hitherto lived a virgin, and doubt nothing but with God's grace I am able so to live still. But if, as my progenitors have done before me, it may please God that I might leave some fruit of my body behind me, I trust you would not only rejoice thereat, but also I know it would be to your great comfort. And on the word of a Queen, I promise you, that if it shall not appear to all the Nobility and Commons, that this marriage shall be for the high benefit and commodity of the whole realm, then will I abstain from marriage while I live.

And now, good subjects, pluck up your hearts, and like true men, stand fast against these rebels, and fear them not, for I assure you, I fear them nothing at all.

(READER B *returns to chair 2. The* BASS *rises and returns the lectern to its previous position*)

(READER C rises, assumes the character of HENRY VIII, and signals with the quill for the SINGERS to come forward. The SINGERS move round the on-stage side of the piano and take up their positions as before while the ACCOMPANIST plays the lead in. They bow to READER C who signals to them to begin, and then sits)

THE HUNT IS UP

TENOR, BARITONE AND BASS

ALL

The hunt is up, the hunt is up,
And it is well nigh day;
And Harry our king is gone hunting
To bring his deer to bay.

BASS

The east is bright with morning light,
And darkness it is fled,
The merry horn wakes up the morn
To leave his idle bed.

TENOR

The horses snort to be at the sport,
The dogs are running free,
The woods rejoice at the merry noise
Of hay-taranta-tee-ree.

BARITONE

The sun is glad to see us clad
All in our lusty green,
And smiles in the sky as he rideth high
To see and to be seen.

ALL

Awake all men, I say again
Be merry as you may:
For Harry our King is gone hunting
To bring his deer to bay.

(READER C dismisses the SINGERS who bow to him and move round the on-stage side of the piano and back to their seats. The BASS sits in chair (a), the BARITONE in chair (b) and the TENOR in chair (c))

(READER C *rises. As he speaks he uses the quill as though correcting a letter he has just written*)

LETTER FROM HENRY VIII TO ANNE BOLEYN

READER C

On turning over in my mind the contents of your last letters, I have put myself into great agony, not knowing how to interpret them, whether to my disadvantage, as you show in some places, or to my advantage, as I understand them in some others; beseeching you earnestly to let me know expressly your whole mind as to the love between us two.

It is absolutely necessary for me to obtain this answer, having been for above a whole year stricken with the dart of love, and not yet sure whether I shall fail of finding a place in your heart and affection, which last point has prevented me for some time past from calling you my mistress. If you please to do the office of a true loyal mistress and friend, and to give yourself body and heart to me, I promise you that not only the name shall be given you, but also that I will take you for my only mistress, casting off all others besides you out of my thoughts and affections, and serve you only.

I beseech you to give an entire answer to this my rude letter, and appoint some place where I may have it by word of mouth, and I will go thither with all my heart. Written by the hand of him who would willingly remain yours, wishing myself (especially of an evening) in my sweetheart's arms, whose pretty duckies I trust shortly to kiss.

(READER C *signs his name with a flourish*)

Henricus Rex

(READER C *puts the quill on the table and returns to chair* 1)

(READER B picks up the quill and writes)

LETTER FROM ANNE BOLEYN TO HENRY VIII

Sir,
READER B

Your Grace's displeasure, and my imprisonment are things so strange unto me, as what to write or what to excuse I am altogether ignorant. For to speak a truth, never a prince had a wife more loyal in all duty and in all true affection, than you have ever found in Anne Boleyn. If then you found me worthy of such honour with your Grace, let not any light fancy or bad council of my enemies withdraw your princely favour from me. Try me, good King; but let me have a lawful trial, and let not my sworn enemies sit as my accusers and judges. Yes, let me receive an open trial. For my truth shall fear no open shame.

But if you have already determined of me, and that not only my death, but an infamous slander must bring you the joying of your desired happiness, then I desire of God, that he will pardon your great sin herein, and that he will not call you to a straight account for your unprincely and cruel usage of me. For at his general judgment seat, where both you and myself must shortly appear, I doubt not, whatsoever the world may think of me, my innocence shall be openly known.

If I have ever found favour in your sight, if ever the name of Anne Boleyn hath been pleasing in your ears, let me obtain this last request. And so I have to trouble your Grace no further, with my earnest prayer to the Trinity to have your Grace in his good keeping, and to direct you in all your actions. From my doleful prison in the Tower, the sixth of May.

Your most loyal and ever faithful wife,

(READER B signs her name)

Anne Boleyn

(READER B puts the quill down on the table)

(The ACCOMPANIST *immediately plays the lead-in to the "Lament for Anne Boleyn". The* TENOR *rises and stands by the upstage centre end of the piano, facing towards* READER B)*

O DEATH, ROCK HER ASLEEP

TENOR

O Death, O Death rock her asleep
Bring her to quiet rest,
Let pass her weary guiltless life
Out of her careful breath.
Toll on thou passing bells,
Ring out her doeful knell,
Let thy sound her death tell.
Death doth draw nigh;
There is no remedy, for she must die.

> *(The* ACCOMPANIST *moves to the piano stool, and the* TENOR *returns to his chair)*

POEM BY HENRY VI *

Kingdoms are but cares,
  State is devoid of stay,
Riches are ready snares,
  and hasten to decay.

Pleasure is a privy prick
  Which vice doth still provoke;
Pomp, imprompt; and fame, a flame;
  Power, a smouldering smoke.

Who meaneth to remove the rock
  Out of the slimy mud,
Shall mire himself, and hardly scape
  The swelling of the flood.

POEM BY HENRY VIII*

As the holly groweth green,
And never changeth hue,
So am I, and e'er have been,
Unto my lady true.

> Green groweth the holly, so doth the ivy,
> Though wintry blasts blow ne'er so high,
> Green groweth the holly.

As the holly groweth green,
With ivy all alone,
When flowers cannot be seen
And greenwood leaves be gone,

Now unto my lady
Promise to her I make,
From all other only
To her I me betake:

Adieu, mine own lady,
Adieu, my special,
Who hath my heart truly,
Be sure, and ever shall.

> Green groweth the holly, so doth the ivy,
> Though wintry blasts blow ne'er so high,
> Green groweth the holly.

POEM BY ELIZABETH*

READER B

When I was fair and young, and favour gracéd me,
Of many was I sought, their mistress for to be;
But I did scorn them all, and answered them therefore,
"Go, go, go, seek some otherwhere!
Importune me no more!"

How many weeping eyes I made to pine with woe,
How many sighing hearts, I have no skill to show;
Yet I the prouder grew, and answered them therefore,
"Go, go, go, seek some otherwhere!
Importune me no more!"

Then spake fair Venus' son, that proud victorious
boy,
And said: "Fine Dame, since that you be-en so coy,
I will so pluck your plumes that you shall say no more,
"Go, go, go, seek some otherwhere!
Importune me no more!"

When he had spake these words, such change grew
in my breast
That neither night nor day since that, I could take
any rest.
Then lo! I did repent that I had said before,
"Go, go, go, seek some otherwhere!
Importune me no more!"

35

POEM BY CHARLES II*

I pass all my hours in a shady old grove,
But I live not the day when I see not my love:
I survey every walk now my Phyllis is gone,
And sigh when I think we were there all alone.
    Oh then 'tis I think there's no hell
    Like loving too well.

But each shade and each conscious bow'r when I find,
Where I once have been happy, and she has been kind,
When I see the print left of her shape on the green,
I imagine the pleasure may yet come again.
    O then 'tis I think no joys are above
    The pleasures of love.

While alone to myself I repeat all her charms,
She I love may be lock'd in another man's arms;
She may laugh at my cares, and so false she may be,
To say all the kind thoughts she before said to me.
    O then 'tis O then, that I think there'e no hell
    Like loving too well.

But when I consider the truth of her heart,
Such an innocent passion, so kind without art;
I fear I have wrong'd her, yet hope she may be
So full of true love to be jealous of me.
    O then 'tis I think that no joys are above
    The pleasures of love.

(The ACCOMPANIST *plays the lead-in. The* SINGERS *rise, move round the off-stage side of the piano, take up a position between it and the harpsichord, and bow to the* READERS *who acknowledge the bow)*

HERE'S A HEALTH UNTO HIS MAJESTY

TENOR, BARITONE AND BASS

ALL	Here's a health unto his Majesty,
BAR.	With a fa la la la la la la,
BASS	Confusion to his enemies,
TEN. & BAR.	With a fa la la la la la la la.
TEN.	And he that will not drink his health,
BAR.	I wish him neither wit nor wealth,
BASS	Nor yet a rope to hang himself,
ALL	With a fa la la la la la la la la la
	With a fa la la la la la la la.

(The SINGERS *bow again to the* READERS *who again acknowledge the bow)*

ALL	All Cavaliers will please combine,
BAR.	With a fa la la la la la la,
BASS	To drink this loyal toast of mine,
TEN. & BAR.	With a fa la la la la la la.
TEN.	And for the man who answers No,
BAR.	I only wish that he may go
BASS	With Roundhead rogues to Jericho,
ALL	With a fa la la la la la la la la la
	With a fa la la la la la la la.

(The SINGERS *move up stage to the bay of the piano and bow again to the* READERS *who rise and face the* SINGERS *and repeat the first verse)*
(As they finish singing the SINGERS *bow low to the* READERS *who also bow low. The whole company then move downstage, form a line, bow and exit left)*

PART TWO

(The MUSICIANS *enter down right; the* READERS *enter down left. They form a line, bow and take their seats as follows:* ACCOMPANIST *on stool at harpsichord,* TENOR *in chair* (*a*), BASS *in chair* (*b*), BARITONE *in chair* (*c*), READER C *in chair* 1, READER B *in chair* 2, READER A *in chair* 3. READER D *sets the lectern in position* (*ii*). READER A *rises and moves to the lectern.* READER D *bows to him and sits in chair* 4)

A COUNTERBLAST TO TOBACCO

READER A

As every human body, dear countrymen, how wholesome soever, is notwithstanding subject to some sorts of diseases, so there is no Commonwealth or Body-Politic that lacks popular errors and corruptions. For remedy whereof, it is the King's to purge it of disease, by Medicines meet for the same.

Now surely in my opinion, there cannot be a more base and hurtful corruption in a country than is the vile use of taking Tobacco in this Kingdom. Now how you are by this custom disabled in your goods, let the gentry of this land bear witness, some of them bestowing three, some four hundred pounds a year upon this precious stink. Is it not both great vanity and uncleanness, that at table, a place of respect, of cleanliness, of modesty, men should not be ashamed, to sit tossing of tobacco pipes and puffing of the smoke of tobacco one to another, to exhale athwart the dishes, and infect the air, when very often men that abhor it are at their repast? Surely smoke becomes a kitchen far better than a dining chamber, and yet it makes a kitchen also oftentimes in the inward parts of men, soiling and infecting them with an unctuous and oily kind of soot, as hath been found in some great tobacco takers, that after their death were opened.

Are you not guilty of sinful and shameful lust? That although you be troubled with no disease, but in perfect health, yet can you neither be merry at an Ordinary, nor lascivious in the Stews, if you lack Tobacco to provoke your appetite to any of those sorts of recreation, lusting after it as the children of Israel did in the wilderness after Quails?

Mollicies and delicacy were the wrack and overthrow, first of the Persian, and next of the Roman Empire. Have you not reason then to be ashamed, and to forbear this filthy novelty, so basely grounded, so foolishly received, and so grossly mistaken in the right use thereof? In your abuse thereof sinning against God, and taking also thereby the marks and notes of Vanity upon you. A custom loathsome to the eye, hateful to the nose, harmful to the brain, dangerous to the lungs, and in the black stinking fume thereof, nearest resembling the horrible Stygian smoke of the pit that is bottomless.

(READER A *moves the lectern to position (iii), moves round behind chairs* 1 *and* 2, *and then sits in chair* 3)

(READER C *rises and takes his place behind the lectern upon which he places his script.* READER D *moves his chair a few feet downstage*)

FROM THE TRIAL OF CHARLES I*

READER D AS LORD PRESIDENT

READER C AS THE KING

LORD PRESIDENT Sir, you have now heard your charge read. It is prayed to the Court, in the behalf of the Commons of England, that you now answer the same.

THE KING I would know by what authority, I mean lawful authority, I was brought hither, and carried from place to place (and I know not what), and when I know what lawful authority I shall answer. Remember I am your King, your lawful King, and what sins you bring upon your heads, and the judgement of God upon this land—think well upon it—I say, think well upon it, before you go further from one sin to a greater.

In the meantime I shall not betray my trust; I have a trust committed to me by God, by old and lawful descent—I will not betray it to answer to a new unlawful authority; therefore resolve me that, and you shall hear of me.

LORD PRESIDENT If you had been pleased to have observed what was hinted to you by the Court at your first coming hither, you would have known by what authority; which authority requires you in the name of the people of England, of which you are elected King, to answer them.

THE KING No, Sir, I deny that.

LORD PRESIDENT If you acknowledge not the authority of the Court, they must proceed.

THE KING England was never an elective kingdom, but an hereditary kingdom for near these thousand years; therefore let me know by what authority I am

43

called hither. I do stand more for the liberty of my people than any here that come to be my lawful judges.

LORD PRESIDENT Sir, how really you have managed your trust, is known. Your way of answer is to interrogate the Court, which beseems not you in your condition.

THE KING I do not come here as submitting to the Court. Yet I will stand as much for the privilege of the House of Commons, rightly understood, as any man here whatsoever. But I see no House of Lords here that may constitute a Parliament. Is this the bringing of the King to his Parliament? Is this the bringing to an end of the treaty in the public faith of the world? Let me see a legal authority warranted by the Word of God, the Scriptures, or warranted by the constitutions of the kingdom, and I will answer.

LORD PRESIDENT Sir, you have propounded a question, and been answered. Seeing you will not answer, the Court will consider how to proceed.

THE KING A king cannot be tried by any superior jurisdiction on earth. If power without law may make laws, I do not know what subject he is in England that can be sure of his life or anything he calls his own. Therefore . . .

LORD PRESIDENT Sir, I must interrupt you, which I would not do, but that what you do is not agreeable to the proceedings of any Court of Justice. You are charged as an high delinquent . . .

THE KING I do not know how a king can be a delinquent; but by any law that I ever heard of, all men—delinquents or what you will—may put in demurrers against any proceeding as legal. I do demand that, and demand to be heard with my reasons: if you deny that, you deny reason.

LORD PRESIDENT You may not demurre the jurisdiction of the Court. They sit here by the authority of the Commons of England, and all your predecessors and you are responsible to them . . .

THE KING I deny that. Show me one precedent.

LORD PRESIDENT Sir, you ought not to interrupt when the Court is speaking to you; this point is not to be debated by you, neither will the Court permit you to do it.

THE KING I say, Sir, by your favour, that the Commons of England was never a Court of Judicature: I would know . . .

LORD PRESIDENT Sir, you are not permitted to go on in that speech or these discourses.

"Charles Stuart, King of England, you have been accused on the behalf of the People of England of high treason and other crimes." The court have determined that you ought to answer the same.

THE KING I will answer the same as soon as I know by what authority you do this.

LORD PRESIDENT If this be all you will say, then gentlemen—you that brought the prisoner hither—take charge of him back again.

THE KING I do require that I may give my reasons why I do not answer.

LORD PRESIDENT Sir, 'tis not for prisoners to require.

THE KING Prisoners? Sir, I am not an ordinary prisoner.

LORD PRESIDENT Sergeant, take away the prisoner.

THE KING Well, Sir, remember the King is not suffered to give his reasons for the liberty and freedom of all his subjects!

LORD PRESIDENT Sir, you are not to have liberty to use this language. How great a friend you have been to the laws and liberties of the people, let all England and the world judge.

THE KING Sir, under favour, it was the liberty, freedom, and laws of the subject that ever I undertook.

LORD PRESIDENT The command of the Court must be obeyed.

(READER D *rises*)

No answer will be given to the charge.

(READER D *sits*)

SENTENCE OF THE HIGH COURT OF JUSTICE UPON CHARLES I

Whereas the Commons of England assembled in Parliament, have authorised and constituted us an High Court of Justice for the trying and judging of Charles Stuart as a tyrant, traitor, murderer and public enemy of the Commonwealth; by virtue whereof the said Charles Stuart hath been three several times convented before this High Court, where a charge of High Treason and other high crimes was exhibited against him, wherein he was charged,

That he, being King of England, out of a wicked design to erect and uphold in himself an unlimited and tyrannical power, hath traitorously and maliciously levied war against the present Parliament and people: and that he hath thereby procured many thousands of the free people of this nation to be slain, many families undone, and many parts of the land spoiled, some of them even to desolation; and that all the said wicked designs and practices were still carried on for the advancement and upholding of the personal interest of himself and his family; and that he thereby hath been and is the occasioner, author, and continuer of the said unnatural, cruel, and bloody wars, treasons, murders, rapines, burnings, spoils, desolations, damage, and mischief to this nation.

Now, therefore, upon serious and mature deliberation of the premises, this Court is fully satisfied in their judgments and consciences, that he is guilty of the wicked designs and endeavours in the said charge set forth.

(READER D *rises*)

For which this Court doth adjudge that he, the said Charles Stuart, as a tyrant, traitor, murderer, and public enemy to the good people of this nation, shall be put to death by the severing of his head from his body.

THE KING Well, Sir.

(READER C *returns to chair* 1. READER D *sits again in chair* 4 *and pushes it back to its original position*)

(*The* Tenor *moves to the on-stage corner of the harpsichord*)

AYRE

Tenor

Mark how the blushful morn in vain
Courts the am'rous marigold;
With sighing blush and weeping rain,
Yet she refuses to unfold.
But when the planet of the day
Approaches with his powerful ray,
Then she spreads, then she receives
His warmer beams within her virgin leaves.

(*The* Tenor *returns to chair (a).
The* Accompanist *closes the harpsichord lid, and moves to the piano stool*)

CHARLES II ON HIS MARRIAGE

READER A

My Lords and Gentlemen of the House of Commons: I will not spend the time in telling you why I called you hither; I am sure I am very glad to see you here.

I will tell you some news that I think will be very acceptable to you. I have been often put in mind by my friends that it was high time to *marry*. But there appeared difficulties enough in the choice, though many overtures have been made to me: and if I should never marry till I could make such a choice against which there could be no inconvenience, you would live to see me an old bachelor, which I think you do not desire to do. I can now tell you, not only that I am resolved to marry, but *whom* I resolve to marry: it is with the daughter of Portugal.

And I tell you with great satisfaction and comfort to myself that after many hours debate in my Privy Council, my Lords, without one dissenting voice (yet there were very few sat silent) advised me with all imaginable cheerfulness to this marriage. Which I looked upon as very wonderful, and even as some instance of the approbation of God Himself; and so I make all the haste that I can to fetch you a Queen hither, who, I doubt not, will bring great blessings with her to you and me.

(READER A *picks up the quill from piano, and moves, with his script down centre*)

49

Portsmouth: May the twenty-first, 1662.

My dear Clarendon,

I arrived here yesterday about two in the afternoon, and as soon as I had shifted myself, I went to my wife's chamber, who I found in bed, by reason of a little cough, and some inclination to a fever, by having certain things stopped at sea which ought to have carried away those humours.

It was happy for the honour of the nation that I was not put to the consummation of marriage last night; for I was so sleepy by having slept but two hours in my journey as I was afraid that matters would have gone very sleepily. I can now only give you an account of what I have seen abed: which in short is, her face is not so exact as to be called a beauty, though her eyes are excellent good, and not anything in her face that in the least degree can shock me. On the contrary, she has as much agreeableness in her looks altogether, as ever I saw: and I have any skill in physiognomy, which I think I have, she must be as good a woman as ever was born.

In a word, I cannot easily tell you how happy I think myself and I must be the worst man living (which I hope I am not) if I be not a good husband.

(Reader A *mimes signing the signature*)

Charles

(Reader A *returns to chair* 3)

Two months later: July 1662.

> (*In the course of writing the next letter* READER A *exchanges looks with* READER B, *who leans over towards him as if she is Lady Castlemaine overlooking what he is writing*)

READER A

My Lord,

I forgot, when you were here last, to desire you not to meddle any more with what concerns *Lady Castlemaine*. I wish I may be unhappy in this world, and in the world to come, if I fail in the least degree of what I have resolved, which is, making my Lady Castlemaine of my wife's bed-chamber.

You know how true a friend I have been to you. If you will oblige me eternally, make this business as *easy* as you can, of what opinion soever you are of, for I am resolved to go through with this matter.

> (READER A *signs with an angry flourish*)

Carolus Rex

> (READER A *puts the quill on the table*)

THE MARQUIS OF HALIFAX
ANATOMISES CHARLES II

READER D

King Charles the Second might more properly be said to have Gifts than Virtues, as Affability and Easiness of Living.

(READER D *rises and moves slowly towards the harpsichord*)

His Affability was a part of his Wit. By his being abroad, he contracted a habit of conversing familiarly which made him very *apt to talk*; perhaps more than a *very nice* judgement would approve. Where wit will run continually, it groweth vulgar: to use it with reserve is very good, and very rare. But he was so good at finding out other men's weak sides that it made him less intent to cure his own: that generally happeneth.

One great objection made to him was the concealing himself, and disguising his thoughts. Those who knew his face, fixed their eyes there, and thought it of more importance to see, than to hear what he said. Princes dissemble with too many not to have it discovered.

(READER D *moves slightly upstage towards* C)

He had not more application to anything than the preservation of his Health. It may be said that his Inclination to *Love* were the effects of Health and a Good Constitution. He had more properly a good stomach to his Mistresses, than any great passion for them, with as little mixture of the *seraphic* part of love as ever man had. I am apt to think his passions stayed as much as any man's ever did in the *lower region*.

This made him like easy mistresses. Mistresses are frequently apt to be uneasy; they are in all respects craving creatures.

(READER D *moves downstage left*

After he was restored, Mistresses were recommended to him, which is no small matter in a Court, where a

Mistress may be very useful to her Friends, not only in the immediate Hours of her Ministry, but by her influences and insinuations at other times. He had wit enough to suspect this, and he had wit enough not to care.

He lived with his Ministers as he did with his Mistresses: he used them, but he was not in love with them. They were to administer Business to him as Doctors do Physic, wrap it up in something to make it less unpleasant.

(READER D *moves slightly upstage towards centre*)

The motive of his giving bounties was to make men less uneasy to him than more easy to themselves. He had not Vigour enough to do a kind thing, much less do a harsh one; but if a hard thing was done to another man, he did not eat his supper the worse for it.

But after all this, when some rough strokes of the Pen have made several parts of the picture look a little hard, it is but Justice to give all due softenings to the less shining parts of his life. He had as good a claim to a kind interpretation as most men. What an angry Philistine would call lewdness, let frailer man call a warmth and sweetness of the blood. If he dissembled, let us remember that he was a King, and that Dissimulation is a Jewel of the Crown. And if he loved too much to lie on the Down-Bed of his Ease, his Subjects had the pleasure during his reign of lolling upon theirs.

(READER D *moves downstage*)

The truth is, the calling of a King, with all its glittering, hath such a weight upon it, that they may rather expect to be lamented than envied. Let his Royal Ashes then lie soft upon him. If all who are akin to his Vices should mourn for him, never Prince would go better attended to his grave.

(READER D *returns to chair* 4. READER C *moves the lectern to position* (*iv*), *and returns to his seat*)

(*As the* ACCOMPANIST *plays the lead-in the* SINGERS
come round the off-stage side of the piano and line up)

THE VICAR OF BRAY

TENOR, BARITONE AND BASS

BASS

In good King Charles' golden days
When loyalty no harm meant,
A zealous High Churchman was I
And so I got preferment.
To teach my flock I never missed,
Kings are by God appointed
And damned are those that dare resist,
Or touch the Lord's annointed.

ALL

And this is the law that I'll maintain
Until my dying day, sir,
That whatsoever King shall reign
I'll be the vicar of Bray sir.

BARITONE

When Royal James obtained the crown
And Popery came in fashion,
The penal laws I hooted down,
And read the Declaration.
The Church of Rome I found would fit
Full well my constitution,
And had become a Jesuit, but for the revolution.

ALL

And this is the law . . . etc.

TENOR

When William was our King declared,
To air our Nation's grievance,
With this new wind about I steered
And swore to him allegiance.
Old principles I did revoke,

Set conscience at a distance;
For Passive Obedience was a joke,
A jest was Non-resistance.
ALL   And this is the law . . . etc.

BASS

When gracious Anne became our Queen
The Church of England's glory,
Another face of things was seen
And I became a Tory.
Occasional Conformists base,
I damned their moderation;
And thought the Church in danger was
By such prevarication.
ALL   And this is the law . . . etc.

BARITONE

When George in pudding-time came o'er
And moderate men looked big, sir,
I turned a cat-in-pan once more
And so became a Whig sir.
And thus preferment I procured
From our new Faith's Defender,
And almost every day abjured the Pope and
  the Pretender.
ALL   And this is the law . . . etc.

TENOR

The Illustrious House of Hanover
And Protestant Succession,
To these I do allegiance swear
While they can keep possession,
For in my faith and loyalty
I never more will falter,
And George my lawful king shall be . . .
   (*The* TENOR *steps forward*)
Until the times do alter.
   (*The* BASS *and* BARITONE *step*
   forward)
ALL   And this is the law . . . etc.
   (*The* SINGERS *return to their seats*
   via the off-stage side of the piano)

55

THE DEATH OF QUEEN CAROLINE*

READER C

I must now as well as I can connect the particulars of the most melancholy fortnight I ever passed in my life.

(READER C rises and moves to the
downstage corner of the harpsichord)

On Wednesday, the 9th of November, the Queen was taken ill and called her complaint the colic. I, imagining her pain to proceed from a goutish humour in her stomach, told her nothing ever gave immediate ease but strong things. To which the Queen replied: "Pshaw! You think that this is the pain of an old nasty stinking gout. But I have an ill which nobody knows of." She then retired, going immediately into bed, where she grew worse every moment.

On Friday the King sent for Ranby the surgeon, and bid him examine her. When he had done so, Ranby went and spoke softly to the King at the chimney, upon which the Queen started up, and said: "I am sure now, you lying fool, you are telling the King I have a rupture." "I am so," said Ranby, "and Your Majesty has concealed it too long." The Queen made no answer, but lay down again, turning her head to the other side, and as the King told me, he thinks it was the only tear he saw her shed whilst she was ill.

I do firmly believe she carried her abhorrence to being known to have a rupture so far that she would have died without declaring it, and though people may think this weakness little of a piece with the greatness of her character, she knew better than anybody else that her power over the King was not preserved independent of the charms of her person.

(READER C moves to left)

During this time the King talked perpetually to me of the irreparable loss her death would be to him. He said that she was the best wife, the best mother, and the best woman that ever was born; and that if she had not been his wife, he had rather have had her for his mistress than any woman he had ever been acquainted with.

On Wednesday morning she sent for Sir Robert Walpole, who saw her alone. As soon as he came out of the room he said: "If ever I heard a corpse speak, it was just now in that room. Oh! My Lord," said he, "If this woman should die, who can tell into what hands the King will fall? Or who will have the management of him?" "For my own part" I replied, "I have not the least doubt how it will be. He will cry for her for a fortnight, forget her in a month, and have two or three women that he will pass his time with to lie with now and then; but whilst they have most of his time, and no power, you will have all the credit, and govern him more absolutely than ever you did."

(READER C *moves upstage a little towards centre*)

About four o'clock the following morning, the Queen complained that her pain was extreme. She then took a ruby ring off her finger, and putting it upon his, said: "This is the last thing I have to give you—naked I came to you, and naked I go from you." She then gave it as her advice, that in case she died, the King should marry again; upon which his sobs began to rise and his tears to fall, and in the midst of this passion, with much ado he got out this answer: "Non—j'aurai—des—maitresses."

The two following days she grew perceptibly weaker every hour. About ten o'clock on Sunday night, the King being in bed and asleep on the floor at the feet of her bed, the Queen began to rattle in the throat. All she said before she died was "I have now got an asthma. Open the window."

(READER C *moves downstage a couple of steps*)

The King kissed the face and hands of the lifeless body several times. The grief he felt for the Queen showed a tenderness of which the world thought him before utterly incapable, and made him for some time more popular and better spoken of than he had ever been before this incident, or than I believe he ever will be again. (READER C *returns to chair* 1)

HORACE WALPOLE ATTENDS THE FUNERAL OF GEORGE II

READER D

A few years later King George II himself died. Horace Walpole attends his funeral in Westminster Abbey.

> (READER A *delivers the first and last two paragraphs of the following piece to the other* READERS, *who respond as if they were eighteenth-century gossips*)

READER A

Do you know, I had the curiosity to go to the burying t'other night. I had never seen a royal funeral; it is absolutely a noble sight. The prince's chamber, hung with purple, and a quantity of silver lamps, the coffin under a canopy of purple velvet, and six vast chandeliers of silver on high stands, had a very good effect. The procession through a line of foot-guards, every seventh man bearing a torch, the horse-guards lining the outside, the drums muffled, the fifes, bells tolling, and minute guns,—all this was very solemn.

> (READER A *rises and moves down centre*)

But the charm was the entrance of the abbey, where we were received by the dean and chapter in rich robes; the whole abbey so illuminated, that one saw it to greater advantage than by day; the tombs, long aisles, and fretted roof, all appearing distinctly, and with the happiest *chiarascuro*.

When we came to the chapel of Henry the Seventh, all solemnity and decorum ceased. No order was observed, people sat or stood where they could or would; the yeomen of the guard were crying out for help, oppressed by the immense weight of the coffin; the bishop read sadly, and blundered in the prayers; the fine chapter, *Man that is born of woman*, was chaunted, not read; and the anthem, besides being immensurably tedious, would have served as well for a nuptial.

This grave scene was fully contrasted by the burlesque Duke of Newcastle. He fell into a fit of crying the moment he came into the chapel, and flung himself back in a stall, the archbishop hovering over him with a smelling-bottle; but in two minutes his curiosity got the better of his hypocrisy, and he ran about the chapel with his glass, to spy who was or who was not there, spying with one hand, and mopping his eyes with the other. Then returned the fear of catching cold; and the Duke of Cumberland, who was sinking with heat, felt himself weighed down, and turning round, found it was the Duke of Newcastle standing upon his train, to avoid the chill of the marble.

(READER A *moves to the piano*)

It was very theatric to look down into the vault where the coffin lay, attended by mourners with lights. Clavering, the groom of the bed-chamber, refused to sit up with the body, and was dismissed by the king's order.

(READER A *crosses behind the readers' chairs, addressing the other* READERS)

The new reign dates with great propriety and decency. Holinshed or Baker would think it begins well. The young King has all the appearance of being amiable. There is extreme good nature, which breaks out on all occasions. He doesn't stand in one spot, with his eyes fixed royally on the ground, and dropping bits of German news: he walks about and speaks to everybody. All his speeches are obliging. If they do as well behind the scenes, as upon the stage, it will be a very complete reign.

(READER A *sits in chair* 3)

FROM THE DIARY OF FANNY BURNEY*

READER B

Well, dear Mrs Delaney beseeched me: "I do beg of you," she said "when the Queen or the King speaks to you, not to answer with mere monosyllables. The Queen often complains to me of the difficulty with which she can get any conversation, as she not only always has to start the subjects, but commonly entirely to support them: and she says there is nothing she so much loves as conversation, and nothing she finds so hard to get." This was a most tremendous injunction; however, I could not but promise her I would do the best I could.

The door of the drawing-room was opened, and a large man, in deep mourning, appeared at it, entering and shutting it himself without speaking. Miss Port, turning round exclaimed: "The King!—Aunt, the King!"

(READER B *rises and moves down centre. She still directs her words partly to the other* READERS; *but now she addresses the audience more directly*)

O mercy! thought I, that I were but out of the room! Which way shall I escape? But before I had taken a single step, the King, in a loud whisper to Mrs Delaney, said: "Is that Miss Burney?" and on her answering "Yes, sir," he bowed, and with a countenance of the most perfect good humour, came close up to me.

"How long have you been come back, Miss Burney?"

"Two days, sir."

60

Unluckily he did not hear me, and repeated his question; and whether the second time he heard me or not, I don't know, but he made a little civil inclination of his head, and went back to Mrs Delaney.

Then he looked at a book of prints on the table. He turned over a leaf or two, and then said:

"Pray, does Miss Burney draw, too?"

The *too* was pronounced very civilly.

"I believe not, sir," answered Mrs Delaney; "at least, she does not tell."

"Oh!" cried he, laughing, "that's nothing! She is not apt to tell; she never does tell, you know! Her father told me that himself. He told me the whole history of her novel 'Evelina'. And I shall never forget his face when he spoke of his feelings at first taking up the book."

Then, coming up close to me, he said:

"But what?—what?—how was it?"

"Sir!" cried I, not well understanding him.

"How came you—how happened it?—what?—what?"

"I—I only write, sir, for my own amusement—only in some odd, idle hours."

"But your publishing—your printing—how was that?"

"I thought—sir—it would look very well in print."

I do really flatter myself this is the silliest speech I ever made. But a fear of laughing made me eager to utter anything.

While this was talking over, a violent thunder was made at the door. I was almost certain it was the Queen. Once more I would have given anything to escape; but in vain.

Miss Port, according to established etiquette on these occasions, opened the door which she stood next, by putting her hand behind her, and slid out backwards into the hall, to light the Queen in.

Immediately seeing the King, the Queen made him a low curtsy and cried:

"Oh! your Majesty is here!"

"Yes," he cried, "I ran here without speaking to anybody."

The Queen made Mrs Delaney sit next her, and Miss Port brought her some tea.

The King, meanwhile, came to me again, and said: "Are you musical?"

"Not a performer, sir."

Then, going from me to the Queen, he cried: "She does not play."

I did not hear what the Queen answered; she spoke in a low voice and seemed much out of spirits.

The King returned to me, and said:

"Are you sure you never play? Never touch the keys at all?"

"Never to acknowledge it, sir."

"Oh! that's it!" cried he; and flying to the Queen, cried: "She does play—but not to acknowledge it!"

The eager air with which he returned to me fully explained what was to follow. I hastily, therefore, spoke first, in order to stop him, crying: "I never, sir, played to anybody but myself! Never!"

(READER B *moves backwards to the piano*)

"No? Are you sure?" cried he, disappointed; "but—but you'll . . ."

"I have never, sir," cried I, very earnestly, "played in my life, but when I could hear nobody else—quite alone, and from a mere love of musical sounds."

There ensued a long silence, and we drank tea.

(READER B *moves behind chair* 1 *and sits in chair* 2. READER C *helps her into her seat*)

Sometime afterwards, the King said he found by the newspapers that Mrs Clive was dead. This led on to the players, and thence to Mrs Siddons.

"I am an enthusiast for her," cried the King, "quite an enthusiast. I think there was never any player in my time so excellent—not Garrick himself; I own it!"

Then, coming close to me, who was silent, he said: "What? What?"—meaning what say you? But I still said nothing.

From players he went to plays, and complained of the great want of good modern comedies, and of the extreme immorality of most of the old ones, till at last he came to Shakespeare.

"Was there ever," cried he, "such stuff as great part of Shakespeare? only one must not say so! But what think you?—What?—Is there not sad stuff? What?—what?"

"Yes, indeed, I think so, sir, though mixed with such excellences that—"

"Oh!" cried he, "I know it is not to be said! but it's true. Only it's Shakespeare, and nobody dare abuse him."

(READER A *rises, moves the lectern to position (v) and sits again.* READER D *moves to the lectern and places his script upon it. He speaks as if giving a lecture*)

W. M. THACKERAY ON GEORGE THE FOURTH

READER D

To make a portrait of George the Fourth at first seemed a matter of small difficulty. There is his coat, his star, his wig, his countenance simpering under it. And yet after reading of him in scores of volumes, hunting him through old magazines and newspapers, having him here at a ball, there at a public dinner, there at races and so forth, you find you have nothing—nothing but a great simulacrum.

His sire and grandsires were men. One knows what they were like: that on occasion they fought and demeaned themselves like tough good soldiers. The sailor King, who came after George, was a man: the Duke of York was a man, big burly, loud, jolly, cursing, courageous.

But this George, what was he? I look through all his life, and try to unswathe and interpret that royal old mummy. I try to take him to pieces, and find silk stockings, padding, stays, a pocket-handkerchief prodigiously scented, one of Truefitt's best nutty-brown wigs reeking with oil, a set of teeth and a huge black stock, under-waistcoats, more under-waistcoats, and then—nothing.

About George one can get at nothing actual. His biographers say that when he commenced housekeeping in that splendid new palace of his, the Prince of Wales had some windy projects of encouraging literature, science, and the arts; of having assemblies of literary characters; and societies for the encouragement of geography, astronomy, and botany. Astronomy,

64

geography and botany—Fiddlesticks! French ballet-dancers, French cooks, horse-jockeys, buffoons, procurers, tailors, boxers, fencing-masters, china, jewel, and gimcrack merchants—these were his real companions.

What a strange court! Shall we cry woe against the open vice and selfishness and corruption? Or look at it as we do at the King in the pantomime, with his pantomime courtiers, whom he pokes with his pantomime sceptre, as he sits down under the guard of his pantomime beefeaters to dine on his pantomime pudding.

It is grave; it is sad: it is a theme most curious for moral and political speculation. The great war of empires and giants goes on. Day by day victories are won and lost by the brave. Torn smoky flags and battered eagles are wrenched from the heroic enemy and laid at his feet; and he sits there on his throne and smiles.

He has been dead now for several years, and one asks how a great society could have tolerated him. *He* the first gentleman of Europe! There is no stronger satire on the proud English society of that day, than that they admired *George*.

(READER D *moves the lectern to position (vi) and returns to his chair*)

(READER B picks up the quill and uses it to write the first three words of the following letter. The letter should be read in the character of an old lady addressing a small boy)

THE REGENCY

READER B

Dear Master Morgan,

I think it's time now for you to write me another letter. Do you write every day. I can show you a big thick copy-book that when I was just your age I wrote for my father. And what do you think he did to reward me? Why, poor old George the Third was coming to summon Parliament. He was a good man and wanted to do right, but he was very obstinate and used to get very angry and at last very ill, and he quite lost his senses and kept calling the people about him peacocks.

When the day came for him to meet his faithful commons, though very ill, he insisted on having his own way, so they gave it him, and he went, and I could see his carriage—all gold and glass, and I did so beg of papa to let me go across Palace Yard, and he carried me across and took me into the House of Commons. And there he was sitting on the Throne with his King's Crown on, his robes scarlet and ermine, and held his speech written out for him, just what he had to say. But, oh dear, he strode up and made a bow and began "My Lords and Peacocks".

The people who were not fond of him laughed, the people who did love him cried, and he went back to be no longer a King, and his eldest son reigned in his stead, and Regent Street was named after him.

(READER B puts the quill on the table)

66

WILLIAM IV'S ACCESSION

Reader C

King George IV had not been dead three days before everybody discovered that he was no great loss, and King William a great gain. Yet never was elevation like that of King William IV. His life has been hitherto passed in obscurity and neglect, surrounded by a numerous progeny of bastards. Nobody ever invited him into their house, or thought it necessary to honour him with any mark of attention or respect. He was in no hurry to take upon himself the dignity of King, nor to throw off the habits and manners of a country gentleman.

(Reader C *moves towards the piano*)

At the late King's funeral he behaved with great indecency. But the ceremony was very well managed, and a fine sight, the military part particularly, and the Guards were magnificent. The attendance was not very numerous, and when they had all got in St. George's Hall a gayer company I never beheld. The King was chief mourner, and, to my astonishment, as he entered the chapel directly behind the body, in a situation in which he should have been apparently, if not really, absorbed in the melancholy duty he was performing, he darted up to Strathaven, shook him heartily by the hand, and then went on nodding to the left and right.

His first speech to the Council was well enough given, but his burlesque character began even then to show itself. He spoke of his brother with all the semblance of feeling, and in a tone of voice properly softened and subdued, but just afterwards, when they gave him the pen to sign the declaration, he said, in his

67

usual tone, "This is a damned bad pen you have given me".

He began immediately to do good-natured things. He has been to Woolwich, inspecting the artillery, to whom he gave a dinner, with toasts and hip, hip, hurrahing and three times three—himself giving the time.

Yesterday he went to the House of Lords, and delivered the Speech very well, they say: but would not wear the crown, which was carried by Lord Hastings. All this was very well—no great harm in it—but when this was over, and he might very well have sat himself quietly down and rested, he must needs put on his plainer clothes and start on a ramble about the streets, alone too! He was soon followed by a mob making an uproar, and when he got near White's a woman came up and kissed him. When he got home he asked them all to go in and take a quiet walk in the garden, and said, "Oh never mind all this; when I have walked about a few times they will get used to it, and will take no notice".

(READER C *moves behind chair* 1)

The other night he had a party, and at eleven o'clock he dismissed them, thus: "Now, ladies and gentlemen, I wish you a good night. I will not detain you any longer from your amusements, and shall go to my own, which is to bed; so come along, my Queen".

(READER C *moves chair* 1 *to the bay of the piano*)

Altogether he seems a kind-hearted, well-meaning, not stupid, burlesque, bustling old fellow, and if he doesn't go mad may make a very decent King. All odd, and people are frightened, but his wits will at least hold till the new Parliament meets.

(READER C *moves behind chairs* 3 *and* 4)

(READER C *remains standing.* READERS A *and* D *remain seated and the three of them form a composed group as·in a Victorian photograph. At the same time the* ACCOMPANIST *plays the lead-in to the Ballad. The* BASS (*or* BARRITONE) *comes forward and bows first to* READER B *and then to the* ACCOMPANIST. READER B *assumes the character of Queen Victoria and acknowledges his bow*)

BALLAD TO AN ABSENT FRIEND

BASS (OR BARITONE)

Hark a whisper o'er the fountain:
Hark a murmur o'er the plain:
Hark a voice from vale and mountain:
Surely 'tis the zephyr's strain.

'Tis the breath of evening stealing
Over field and over grove,
Breathing sounds of gentlest feeling,
Sounds of transport, sounds of love,
Sounds of transport, sounds of love.

> (*The* BASS (*or* BARITONE) *bows to* READER B *and returns to his seat.* READER B *rises;* READER C *sits in chair* 2)

(READER B *moves towards the harpsichord. The*
SINGER *seated in chair (a) moves the harpsichord stool
to on-stage of the harpsichord, bows to* READER B, *and
returns to his seat. Extra light comes up on* READER B
and light fades on the READERS' *chairs*)

FROM QUEEN VICTORIA'S PRIVATE JOURNALS

READER B

June the twenty-eighth, 1838.

> (READER B *sits on the harpsichord
> stool facing right and places her script
> on the lid of the instrument, which she
> treats as a desk*)

I was awoke at four o'clock by the guns in the Park.
Got up at seven, feeling strong and well. I dressed,
having taken a little breakfast before I dressed and a
little after.

At ten I got into the state coach, and we began our
Progress. It was a fine day, and the crowds of people
exceeded what I had ever seen. Their good humour
and excessive loyalty was beyond everything, and I
really cannot say *how* proud I feel to be the Queen of
such a nation.

I reached the Abbey amid deafening cheers at a
little past half past eleven. There I found my eight
train-bearers. After putting on my mantle, and the
young ladies having properly got hold of it, I left the
robing-room and the Procession began. The Bishop of
Durham stood on the side near me, but he was, as Lord
Melbourne told me, remarkably *maladroit*, and could
never tell me what was to take place. At the beginning
of the Anthem, I retired to St Edward's chapel, and put
on the supertunica of cloth of gold. I then proceeded
bare-headed into the Abbey. The Crown being placed

70

on my head, was, I must own, a most beautiful impressive moment.

My excellent Lord Melbourne, who stood close to me throughout the whole ceremony, was *completely* overcome at this moment, and very much affected. He gave me *such* a kind, and I may say *Fatherly* look.

The Enthronization and the Homage of, first, all the Bishops, and then my Uncles, and lastly of all the Peers, in their respective order, was very fine. It's a pretty ceremony: they first all touch the Crown, and then kiss my hand. Poor old Lord Rolle, who is eighty-two, and dreadfully infirm, in attempting to ascend the steps fell and *rolled* quite down, but was not the least hurt. When Lord Melbourne's turn to do Homage came, there was loud cheering. When he knelt down, he pressed my hand, and I grasped his with all my heart, at which he looked up: his eyes filled with tears and he seemed much touched; as he was, I observed, throughout the ceremony.

After the homage was concluded, I descended from the Throne, and repaired to St Edward's Chapel, as it is called, but which, as Lord Melbourne said, was more unlike a chapel than anything he had ever seen; for what was *called* an *Altar* was covered with sandwiches, bottles of wine, etc.

The Archbishop came in and *ought* to have delivered the Orb to me, but I had already got it, and he (as usual) was *so* confused and puzzled and knew nothing, and—went away. Here we waited for some minutes and Lord Melbourne took a glass of wine. The Procession being formed, I replaced my Crown (which I had taken off for a few minutes), took the Orb in my left hand and the sceptre in my right, and thus *loaded*, proceeded through the Abbey, which resounded with cheers. At about half-past four I re-entered my carriage, and arrived home a little after six.

At eight we dined. I sat between Uncle Ernest and

Lord Melbourne who was much affected in speaking of the whole ceremony. He asked kindly if I was tired. I said that the Crown hurt me a good deal and that I felt a little tired on my feet. We spoke of the numbers of Peers at the Coronation, which, Lord Melbourne said, with the tears in his eyes, was unprecedented. I observed that there were very few Viscounts; he said there *are* very few Viscounts; that they were an odd sort of title and not really English; that Dukes and Barons were the only real English titles; that Marquises were likewise not English and that they made people Marquises when they did not wish to make them Dukes.

We then spoke of the Pages, who were such a nice set of boys, and who were so handy. Little Lord Stafford and Lord Mountcharles were pages to their fathers and looked lovely; Lord Paget (not a fine boy) was Lord Melbourne's page and remarkably handy, he said.

When I spoke of my intending to go to bed, etc., he turned round to me with tears in his eyes, and said *so* kindly, "You must be very tired.

(*The* ACCOMPANIST *begins to play "God Save the Queen" very gently*)

You did it beautifully—every part of it, with so much taste. It's a thing you can't give a person advice upon; it must be left to a person." To hear this from this kind impartial friend, gave me great and real pleasure.

(READER B *rises*)

I shall ever remember this day as the *Proudest* of my life.

(READER B *moves slowly back to chair 1. She should time her move so that she is seated by the time the* ACCOMPANIST *finishes playing "God Save the Queen". She then nods to him and signals for him to continue.*)

VARIATIONS ON "GOD SAVE THE QUEEN"

(When he has finished, the ACCOM-
PANIST *bows to* READER B *and
sits again at the piano.* READERS C
and D *move their chairs in on either
side of* READER A *so that the three
of them are close together)*

(Light comes up on chairs 2, 3 *and* 4, *and fades on the
rest of the stage)*

EPILOGUE
From "THE MORTE D'ARTHUR"

READER A AS NARRATOR
READER C AS KING ARTHUR*
READER D AS SIR BEDIVERE*

NARRATOR And thus they fought all the long day
until it was near night, and by that time was there an
hundred thousand lay dead upon the down. Then
the noble King Arthur, being wounded unto death,
looked about him and said:

KING ARTHUR Jesu mercy! Where are all my noble
knights become? Alas that I should ever see this
doleful day, for now I am come to mine end.

NARRATOR Then the King fell in a swoon to the
earth, and Sir Bedivere, the last of all his knights,
led him weakly and with great mourning, to a little
chapel not far from the sea-side.

KING ARTHUR Now leave this mourning and weeping, gentle knight,

NARRATOR Said the king,

KING ARTHUR For all this will not avail me. For my time passeth on fast. Therefore, take thou here Excalibur, my good sword, and go with it to yonder water's side, and when thou comest there, I charge thee throw my sword in that water, and come again and tell me what thou seest there.

NARRATOR So Sir Bedivere departed. And by the way he beheld that noble sword, that the pommel and haft was all precious stones. And then he said to himself:

SIR BEDIVERE If I throw this rich sword in the water, thereof shall never come good, but harm and loss.

NARRATOR So he hid Excalibur under a tree, and came again unto the king, and said he had been at the water and had thrown the sword into the water.

KING ARTHUR What saw thou there?

NARRATOR Said the King.

SIR BEDIVERE Sir,

NARRATOR He said,

SIR BEDIVERE I saw nothing but waves and winds.

KING ARTHUR That is untruly said of thee,

NARRATOR Said the king,

KING ARTHUR And therefore go thou lightly again, and do my commandment.

NARRATOR Then Sir Bedivere returned again, and yet him thought sin and shame to throw away that noble sword. And so efte he hid the sword, and returned again, and told the king that he had been at the water and done his commandment.

KING ARTHUR What sawest thou there?

NARRATOR Said the king.

SIR BEDIVERE Sir,

NARRATOR He said,

SIR BEDIVERE I saw nothing but the waters wappe and waves wanne.

KING ARTHUR Ah, traitor unto me and untrue!

NARRATOR Said King Arthur.

KING ARTHUR Now has thou betrayed me twice! Thou art named a noble knight, and would betray me for the riches of this sword. But now go again lightly; for thy long tarrying putteth me in great jeopardy of my life, for I have taken cold.

NARRATOR Then Sir Bedivere departed, and went to the sword, and lightly took it up, and went unto the water's side. And there he threw the sword as far into the water as he might. And there came an arm and an hand above the water and met it, and caught it, and so shook it thrice and brandished, and then vanished away with the sword into the water. So Sir Bedivere came again to the king, and told him what he saw.

KING ARTHUR Alas,

NARRATOR Said the king,

KING ARTHUR Help me hence, for I dread me I have tarried over long.

NARRATOR Then Sir Bedivere took the king upon his back, and so went with him to the water's side. And by the bank hoved a little barge with many fair ladies in it, and all they had black hoods.

KING ARTHUR Now put me into that barge.

NARRATOR Said the king. And so he did softly; and there received him three ladies with great mourning. And in one of their laps King Arthur laid his head. And anon they rowed from the land, and when Sir Bedivere beheld all those ladies go from him, he cried:

SIR BEDIVERE Ah, my lord Arthur, my King, what shall become of me, now ye go from me?

KING ARTHUR Comfort thyself,

NARRATOR Said the king,

KING ARTHUR And do as well as thou mayest, for in

75

me is no trust for to trust in. For I will into the vale of Avilion to heal me of my grievous wound. And if thou hear never-more of me, pray for my soul.

NARRATOR And as soon as Sir Bedivere had lost sight of the barge, he wept and wailed, and so took to the forest; and so he went all that night.

> (READER A *rises and moves down centre. All light fades out except a spot on* READER A)

*Thus of Arthur I find no more written; neither more of the very certainty of his death heard I never read. Yet some men say in many parts of England that King Arthur is not dead, but had by the will of our Lord Jesu into another place: and men say that he shall come again. I will not say that it shall be so, but rather I would say, here in this world, he changed his life. But many men say that there is written upon his tomb this verse:

HIC JACET ARTHURUS REX, QUONDAM REX QUE FUTURUS. . . . The Once and Future King.

> (READER A *opens his arms and steps backwards as the Light fades to Black Out.*
>
> *The Lights come up again immediately. The* READERS *come forward and bow. They then turn upstage and applaud the* MUSICIANS, *who rise and bow. The* COMPANY *then bow together and exit—the* MUSICIANS *right; the* READERS *left. For Curtain calls they return and form a line down centre, and bow twice*)